Edmund's Tale
Growing up with disabilities

BY MOLLY MERROW

Second Edition

(First Edition printed October, 1996)

Newspaper photo reprinted courtesy of Nashoba Publications

Photograph of pet show by Arlene Trollope

All other photographs by Molly Merrow

Copyright © 2013 Molly Merrow

All rights reserved

ISBN-10: 0988943700

ISBN-13: 978-0-9889437-0-4

(paperback, perfect-bound)

Foreword

I have spent years in education as a teacher, consultant and administrator and as I grew in my profession I came to realize that accommodations should just be a natural part of instruction and life. When I taught classes in the Curriculum and Instruction Department at the University of Iowa I wanted the students to see how making simple accommodations and providing support can help a child be a part of the world in which they live. During that time I came across *Edmund's Tale* because I knew Molly Merrow's mother and she knew that I worked in special education.

Edmund's Tale is a delightful story of some kittens and two young children, which is not that uncommon in children's stories, but I found myself drawn to the story for its simple yet poignant illustration of what I had been talking about for years.

I was able to acquire multiple copies of the book to give to colleagues in education as well as future educators so they, too, could see the brilliance of what small things can do to help lead someone to greater independence, joy and a sense of satisfaction. Edmund demonstrates this very well by taking us beyond the soft, sweetness of the kitten to determination, strength and ingenuity that develops a full character with a most positive attitude toward life, love and support.

Jeanie Wade-Nagle
Early Education Supervisor
Grant Wood Area Education Agency
Iowa City, IA

My name is Edmund and this is the story of how I grew up.

I guess I've always been different, but that's okay.

Everyone should be different in some way or other,

or they wouldn't be who they are.

When people meet me, they can see that I'm different.

I was born that way.

My mom, Noel, had been adopted by Robin and Sally.

Soon after she came to live with them,

Noel presented her new family with four new kittens.

They say my big brother Nat was born first. He was silver and white and very strong. Next was my sister Monica, a roly poly gray tiger cat.

Then I arrived. I was silver with a white ring around my neck. Sally says my cute little crooked tail was the first thing she noticed about me. Last was my brother Tadalique. He was silver too, and so tiny. We were born with our eyes and ears shut tight because that's how newborn kittens are.

Mother Noel licked each of us all over. We cried but she just kept licking. Then we got hungry. The others were sucking, getting lots of our mother's milk, but I couldn't eat. I don't know why. Sally says I just cried and wriggled around like I was looking for something. Sally tells me I was awfully noisy. I must have been really hungry.

Sally put some special kitten milk into a tiny baby bottle

just big enough for a doll.

She fed me that way.

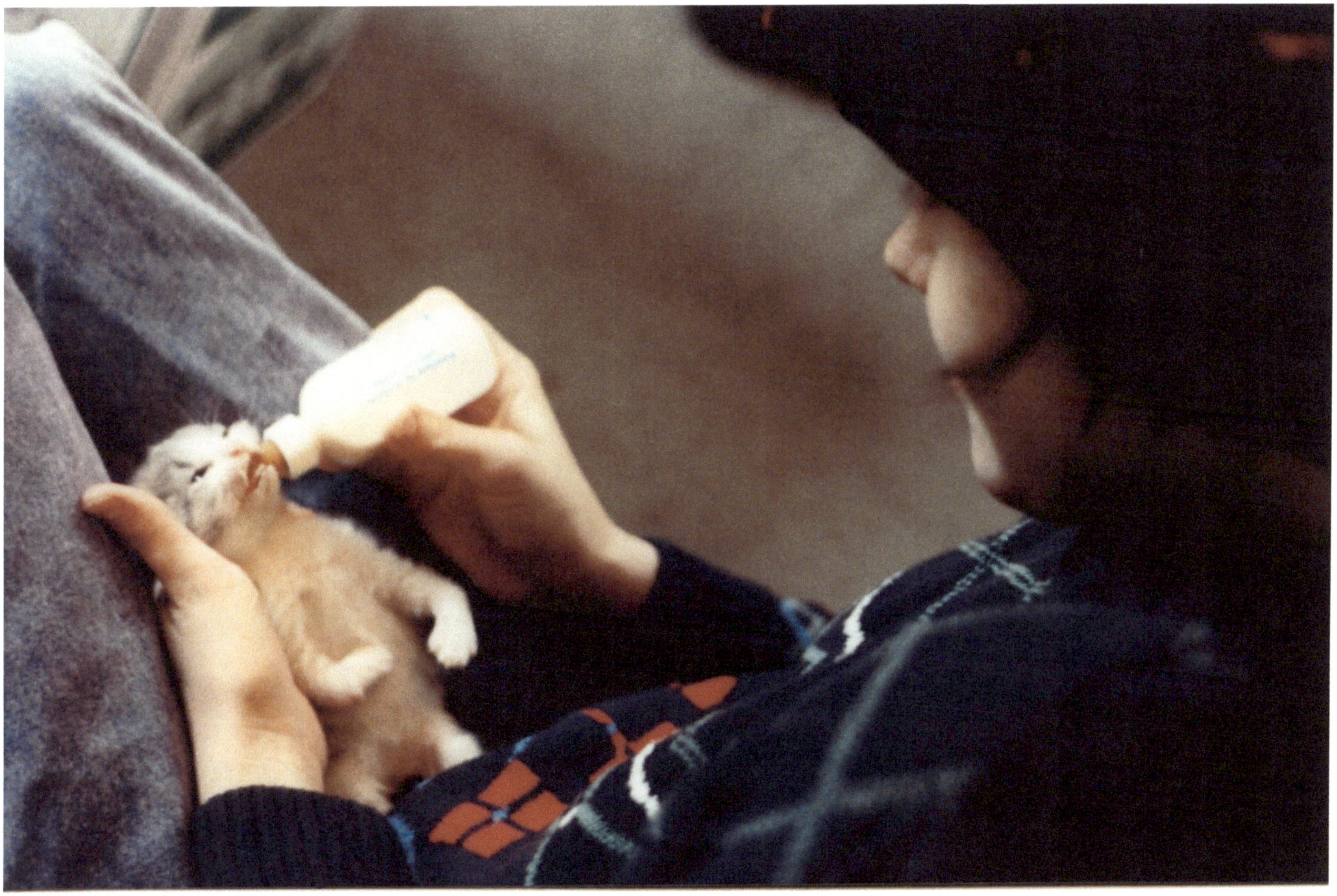

Sally decided that I was her baby. Because I was born in the wintertime, she sometimes wrapped me up in a pink dolly's quilt to keep me warm.

Whenever I was hungry, she fed me my bottle. I couldn't suck very well, so she had to squeeze the milk into my mouth. Sometimes the milk spilled all over my fur, but Sally always made sure that I got plenty to eat.

Mother Noel licked me clean after Sally put me back into the box.

My front paws were different from the other kittens, kind of short and twisted.

I had trouble holding myself up when I was little.

I kind of liked getting so much attention from Sally and Robin,

but I know that they were worried about me.

When we were about 10 days old, Sally tells me, our eyes opened up.

I didn't know it then, but my eyes didn't work well.

Everything was blurry.

Even though I couldn't hold myself up,

I wiggled around to get anywhere I wanted to go.

We lived in a box when we were little.

Mother Noel kept us warm, and we were happy just being together.

My little brother Tadalique was my best friend.

Whenever Sally picked me up to feed me, Tadalique cried to be picked up too.

I was taken out of the box a lot.

Sally and Robin played with me, fed me, and gave me lots of kisses.

They played with the other kittens, but I seemed to get the most attention.

Sometimes I cried, and Mother Noel would come try to carry me back to the box.

She wanted all of her kittens in one place.

I learned to crawl, but it was hard to hold myself steady on my short front paws. I kept practicing, though, and sure enough, I got so I could wobble around the box pretty well.

Because one of my paws was so short and twisted, I couldn't walk straight ahead, but went in circles, round and round. I cried, but then I had to try again.

I found that if I put my front paws together, they were strong enough to hold me up. I invented my own way of walking.

When the other kittens started climbing out of the box, Sally cut a little door in the cardboard so I could get out, too. It was fun to play with the other kittens, and I liked exploring the world.

Robin carried me around wherever he went.

I liked to curl up in his lap when he did his homework or watched television, and he hugged me a lot. He tried to teach me how to do things, like walk and jump and climb the stairs.

I watched the other kittens playing on the steps but I couldn't climb. I was sad because I could tell that they were having fun.

Besides, I wanted to find out what was at the top of the stairs.

I couldn't go up even one step because it was so hard, so I sat at the bottom and cried.

Robin showed me how to dig my claws into the carpet and lift myself up to the next step. It was such a long way to the top. While Nat and Monica and Tadalique were running up and down the steps in a flash, I had to work so hard to just climb one step. I didn't give up, though. Every day I practiced. I dug my claws into everything I could find.

As I got bigger and stronger, the stairs seemed to get smaller.

Soon it wasn't so hard.

One day I made it to the top of the steps.

Then I was able to explore the rooms upstairs.

I liked that.

I found Robin's bunk bed and thought that maybe someday I could even climb up there for a nap.

Monica and Nat were soon old enough to go to new homes.

Robin cuddled the four of us in the chair we were born in before my big brother and big sister went to their new families.

Tadalique and I stayed with Sally and Robin and our mom, Noel.

As we got older, Tadalique and I grew gray stripes. Tadalique's eyes changed to yellow, and he could see everything pretty clearly, even in the dark. My eyes stayed blue and round, and I couldn't see very well at all.

For me, the world is filled with mist and sparkles and lights and shadows.

By using my ears and nose and whiskers, though, I can tell what is happening and where things are.

I'm glad I can see well enough to chase bugs, because that's fun.

I've always had shiny Christmas things as toys because I can see the sparkles.

Catnip mice are fun too, because they smell so good.

Cats love jumping up onto furniture and counters, and I wanted to do that too.

It took me a little longer to figure out how to jump up and land, though.

When I really wanted to get up onto a chair, sometimes I would cry and Sally or Robin would lift me up.

I wanted to do it myself, though, so I kept working at it.

My front paws were not very strong, but I learned how to spring using my back legs.

Even though I had a kinky stub of a tail, I could balance better than Tadalique, and I found it easy to stand up.

I have always been a talker, and when I wanted to be held, I could stand up, hold up my front paws and ask in my best begging voice.

"Meow, meow, meow. Please pick me up."

Sally always scooped me up.

--- ---

After I learned how to jump up onto the furniture, Tadalique and I found some great places to nap. We loved to curl up together in a sunny spot on the back of the chair that we were born in. Kittens love to take cat naps.

My paws get tired easily, so I have a habit of just plopping over on my side to take a rest. Robin thought that was cute and started to call me Ploppy. Sometimes he calls me Ploppadiddler. Sally calls me Eddie. I have lots of cute nicknames that Robin and Sally use because they love me. I know I wouldn't like mean nicknames about things I can't do, or about how I'm different.

Sally and Robin gave me lots of kisses, right on the mouth.

Sometimes I liked it, but sometimes I didn't.

I often would wake up Sally in the morning with a little kiss, just to let her know that it was time to fix me my breakfast.

Sometimes she liked it, but sometimes she didn't.

I guess she likes to sleep later than I do.

She doesn't take naps during the day like cats do.

After breakfast I would always lick my fur clean.

My mother taught me that.

Then I would curl up and watch Sally and Robin get ready for school.

I didn't have to go to school.

I learned what cats need to know from my mother Noel.

Tadalique and I were always together, sometimes playing and fighting, but we liked sleeping curled up together in Robin's lap the best.

Tadalique wasn't so little anymore, and protected me from the other cats even though I could take care of myself, I'm sure.

Like other babies, Tadalique and I had to get shots from the doctor.

After one of my visits to my doctor, I came down with a fever.

I was so cranky I didn't want to play.

I didn't even want to be held.

I climbed on top of a big soft mouse doll to wait until I felt better.

My mom Noel knew I was feeling sick,

so she tried to comfort me.

She licked me as I fell asleep.

I know Sally and Robin were worried about me,

but the next day I woke up feeling much better.

I am usually a well behaved little cat, but sometimes Tadalique and I get into trouble.

We just can't help it.

There was one time when Sally brought home some flowers for the table.

I could smell the blossoms and the ferns, and it had a tempting shiny silver ribbon, too.

There it was, sitting on the kitchen table, smelling very interesting.

Tadalique and I couldn't resist.

I had to stand on my tiptoes to reach those delicious flowers and rip out the ferns. We got a little carried away, and chewed up most of the flowers.

Finally we knocked the whole thing onto the floor.

The next morning, Sally saw what we had done.

"You naughty boys," she scolded, and then she cleaned up the mess.

We really were sorry, but we did have lots of fun with those flowers.

I wish Sally would bring home some more flowers.

When Christmas came, it was almost our first birthday, and we were all grown up.

Sally put up the Christmas tree, and had some new ornaments made with our names.

Mine was shaped like a Christmas tree and Tadalique's was shaped like a stocking.

I loved playing with the shiny decorations and taking a cat nap under the tree.

Sally said I was the best Christmas present she ever got.

I usually stay at home, but one day, Sally and Robin took me for a ride to a pet show in the town park. Everywhere were bunnies and ducks, puppies and guinea pigs and even a pony. I was to be in the pet show!

When the judges came around, they asked Robin about my special qualities. Robin said I am one of a kind, and very brave and clever.

The judges remarked on my lovely soft coat, (I do take special care of my fur), and they admired my adorable little tail and my beautiful blue eyes.

I was so proud that I had won a first place blue ribbon as "best cat in show."

A newspaper photographer took my picture with the blue ribbon.

Sally put my blue ribbon on the wall where everyone could see it.

I was tired after a long day and glad to be back with my brother Tadalique.

I know that I always have to try harder to do the same things that Tadalique and the other cats can do.

Sometimes I have to do things differently, but I always keep trying.

Maybe I'll never catch a mouse or play outside, but I know how to stand up, I know how to talk in my own cat way, and I can give kisses.

I can even climb up to the top of Robin's bunk bed.

Life is full of fun things to do, and so many things to learn.

I don't mind being different.

I like being who I am.

I'm Edmund and I'm special.

Acknowledgements

This book would not be possible without the tender loving care shown by Robin and Sarah, the children who helped to raise Edmund. Thank you Corinna for rescuing and bringing home Mama Noel.

I greatly appreciate the input and support of the late Norm Tucker as well as other members of the Ayer Rotary Club who gave me direction through focus groups and personal encouragement.

I want to thank the students of Florence Roche Elementary School in Groton, Massachusetts for their inspiration. When I visited their classrooms to write a newspaper feature story on student authors, I came away determined to write *Edmund's Tale*. If these students could write such clever and magnificent books, I had to try to follow their example.

I also received essential advice from my friends and co-workers at Nashoba Publications.

Most of all I would like to thank my mother Carol Considine, a retired elementary school special needs teacher, who persuaded me to write the first edition, and urged me to publish this new color edition. She is certain that many children will be inspired by Edmund's spirit.

~ Molly Merrow

www.ingramcontent.com/pod-product-compliance
Lightning Source LLC
Chambersburg PA
CBHW041538040426
42446CB00002B/141